50 YEARS OF CARNEGIE HALL

ARTHUR ALLAN

CONTENTS

FOREWORD

The Carnegie Dunfermline Trust is very happy to sponsor the publication of this book commemorating the first 50 years of Carnegie Hall. Although for the last 25 years the Hall has been managed by the local Council, it was the Trustees who built it — and ran it for almost exactly half of its life so far.

The Hall is of course a prominent landmark on the skyline of Dunfermline, and it has been a considerable influence on the lives of many local people, whether as performers on its stage or as members of its audiences. Like most halls, it has a fascinating story to tell — and Arthur Allan has produced a lively account of the people and events, the incidents and characters who have contributed to that story.

The Trustees hope this book will remind Dunfermline people how fortunate they are to have such a fine Hall. They wish it and its management every success in the future.

Walter Hutchison,
Chairman
Carnegie Dunfermline Trust

When the full history of the Carnegie Dunfermline Trustees' proposed new concert hall is written it should constitute a very curious document indeed.

**Leader Column,
Dunfermline Press,
October 1932.**

Carnegie Hall? Oh yes, I know Carnegie Hall ... that was my first reaction when asked to write this book. That's the place I used to take my daughter for her dancing classes.

Wrong! That's the Music Institute, I was told quite sternly. Carnegie Hall is the bigger building next door, the one with the Tiffany Window in the west wall.

Tiffany Window? I didn't even know what a Tiffany Window was, far less that Dunfermline boasted one. I was not alone. My knowledge was on a par with the rest of the citizenry of Andrew Carnegie's home town. In the next few months I learned an awful lot about the place. Hopefully enough to make reading this book not just instructive but entertaining too.

As you can imagine, reaching such heights of knowledge from such humble beginnings couldn't have been done without help. Nor could it have been done by months of poring over musty record books. It needed the touch of people who knew the place when it was first opened in 1937, and others who have been involved in its story in the ensuing 50 years.

I couldn't begin to list all the good folk who willingly gave of their time to recall the happy days and the sad days. Every single one of them added a little piece to my overall picture. Many of them were only too happy to entrust to my care precious personal and irreplaceable photographs. My thanks to them all.

Special thanks are due to the Carnegie Dunfermline Trust for inviting me to compile the book: to the Trust's Secretary, Fred Mann, and his staff: to Jim McIsaac and Bobby Nicholson for giving me the run of the place while I took notes and photographs: to Chris Neale and the staff of the town's Reference Library: to editor Bill Livingstone and the Dunfermline Press for finding cuttings and pictures: to Isaac Stern, Alastair Duncan, Gino Francesconi and Alice Cooney Frelinghuysen in New York: and to the Carnegie Youth Theatre youngsters who braved a freezing cold morning on the steps of the Hall so that we could get a colourful cover picture to contrast with the line-up for the opening ceremony 50 years earlier.

Old pictures I delved through for this book bore the stamps of such stalwarts of the local photographic scene as Norval, Morris Allan and Peter Leslie, as well as the Dunfermline Press. I am indebted to Christopher Copner for his picture of the Tiffany Window and Scotsman Publications in Edinburgh for the photos of Russell Hunter, Isaac Stern and Harry Lauder.

Pictures were loaned to me by Vince Hill, John Smith, Elizabeth Wright, Audrey Mortimer, Jimmy Hunter, Alex Wallace, Mary Wynne, Carnegie Dunfermline Trust and Dunfermline District Council. The American pictures are by courtesy of Carnegie Hall, New York.

I've enjoyed putting this story together. I hope you enjoy reading it. And if you do enjoy the book, why not go along and see the show!

Arthur Allan

BUILDINGS meant to last: the Music Institute, once the house of Benachie, on the left and what was once planned as its concert and practice hall, the pillared frontage of the Carnegie Hall on the right.

1

FIRE! FIRE!

For Mike Pendlowski, March 21st 1980 was a day of mixed emotions. As stage manager of Dunfermline Gilbert & Sullivan Society, he'd had his share of the offstage dramas an audience never sees. For example, curtains that wouldn't close properly when a cable jumped off a drum: fixed with just hours to spare. And the weather had been less than kind, keeping early-week audiences below what might have been expected.

Now it was Saturday. One more opening, one final curtain call, and The Gondoliers would be back on dry land, the G & S show over for another year. Standing in the Ducal Palace set, Mike peered through the harsh stage lights towards the 600 seats he hoped soon to see completely filled. Last nights are traditionally good houses among the amateur companies who make so much successful use of Carnegie Hall.

Now it was 2.15 in the afternoon. Only one person was in the auditorium, a photographer making a record of sets which, for the first time, had been hired. Usually the Society built their own.

Suddenly Mike was aware of movement, off to the right and about ten feet above stage level. Horrified, he watched the spotlight beams catch and hold a thin spiral of smoke drifting towards the roof. In a split second the smoke grew thicker and there was a quick flash of flame. The curtains were on fire...

With so much electrical equipment around, the only extinguisher that could be used was CO_2 ... and that had no chance of reaching even the base of the flames, now licking up the curtains.

Quickly Mike dropped the safety curtain and closed the side doors, containing the blaze within the stage area, then dashed to the pay phone in the corridor. The photographer was already dialling 999 from a shop in the East Port.

As Mike rushed outside, he could hear the sirens of the fire engines as they came racing through the big doors of the Fire Station just a few hundred yards along Carnegie Drive.

INSIDE the Fire Station, Blue Watch scrambled aboard two fire engines and a turntable, learning as they pulled on their gear that Carnegie Hall was their destination. Within seconds they were circling Sinclair Gardens roundabout and could see smoke escaping from under the Hall's eaves. Another appliance was immediately called in from Rosyth as back-up.

SOMEWHERE on the road between Inverkeithing and Dunfermline, deputy stage manager John Longmuir glanced in his mirror and saw flashing blue lights coming up behind him, sweeping past in a howl of sirens.

'I wonder where they're going', he remarked to his wife, Meg. The Longmuirs were heading for Carnegie Hall to help get things ready for the evening ... and a show that would never take place.

CARETAKER Bobby Nicholson had already been to the Hall that day, to the Saturday morning children's club where they'd been showing films on a screen at the front of the stage. At 2.15 he was at home relaxing before he returned to welcome patrons for the performance.

Mike Pendlowski had asked the police to contact him and Bobby rushed up the town. As he turned the corner his heart missed a beat; there seemed to be fire engines all over the place.

TOM ALLAN, the Hall's official fireman, whose job it was to keep an eye on safety during performances, was also preparing for the night's show when a friend rushed in to tell him that the place had been 'burned to the ground'. He grabbed his coat and quickly made his way towards the Hall.

FIREMEN rushed hose reels through the big side door into the props room. Others worked their way along to the far side of the Theatre, outside the fire curtain. When the stage doors were opened, the blaze would be attacked from both sides at once.

WHEN it was first opened the Carnegie Hall ranked as one of the best-equipped halls in Scotland. Now completely redecorated and fitted with top-class lighting and sound equipment, it's a title it could still lay claim to in the 1990s.

The fire by this time had run right up the curtain and spread along the hanging scenery, dropping burning debris over the stage. High above, bits of the ceiling had caught alight. Jets of water were hitting the sides of the wooden joists but failing to get through to where flames were licking around electrical cables.

Station Officer George Hogg spotted the danger and two men were despatched, wearing breathing apparatus, up the vertical ladders at the side of the stage, to get above the danger area.

Soon the flames were out and firemen went up into the ceiling area, opening the rooflights, spaced out about every ten yards or so, letting the choking smoke escape.

MIKE PENDLOWSKI slowly sipped a cup of tea as he scanned the Hall for signs of what was happening inside. He was still very shocked … he must have been, for if there's one thing he hates it's tea!

Bobby Nicholson and Tom Allan stood together, in tears at what was happening to their beloved Theatre.

The blaze was put out quickly, but it was four hours before the fire services declared the Hall safe. Inside, Mike found the place not looking as bad as he had feared. Firemen had cleared the debris to the back of the stage but the area was saturated with water and the drapes and parts of the stage area looked in a sorry state.

By now members of the G & S Society had heard about the disaster and initiated a chain of phone calls telling other members and ticketholders that there would be no show. Town shops broadcast the news on their tannoy systems and Radio Forth spread the word further afield.

Bobby Nicholson offered the firemen a cup of tea and a little sustenance for their efforts, realising just in time that all he could give them was crisps … smoky bacon flavour!

He also took a phone call from a woman wanting to know what the big picture would be next time they put on a film show.

'Towering Inferno,' snapped back a man under a lot of stress, and was a little disconcerted the next evening when the said lady turned up to book tickets.

She hadn't heard a thing about the fire and a chastened Bobby had to explain, apologise, and get her a taxi home.

The G & S party went ahead as planned, in the Annexe, but it seemed more like a wake, members taking little comfort in dark jokes about the local newspaper billing the show as 'sparkling'.

By 9 o'clock the undamaged scenery was on the road back to London and Mike Pendlowski dumped the clothes he'd been wearing throughout the drama into a bin, still smelling of smoke.

The blaze hadn't been a big one but the damage was considerable. Everything that had been on the stage or above it had been affected by flames, smoke or water. Station Officer Hogg had been pleased to find the fire curtain down, keeping the blaze within the sealed 'box' of the stage. In fact, so tight was that seal that even the smell of smoke wasn't detected within the seating area for three or four days.

The Hall had been saved and went on to reach its half century seven years later. Something a lot of people would not have put their money on back in the twenties when a concert hall project was first discussed.

In fact the much more grandiose plans of that time were all scrapped. The REAL Carnegie Hall, the vast concert hall planned to rival anything in Britain, was never built at all…

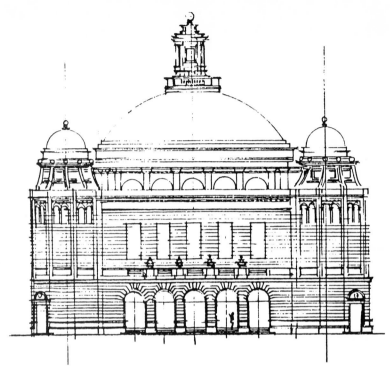

ONE of the grand designs for a proposed music hall to be sited within Pittencrieff Park. At one time the hall was planned for a site near the gate on to Pittencrieff Street, at another for the spot where the Andrew Carnegie statue now stands.

HALF a century before Carnegie's home-town hall finally came into being, he had paid for the construction of this huge building on the corner of New York's Seventh Avenue. Eventually Carnegie Hall became one of the world's great centres for music of every kind. This picture was taken in 1895, four years after it was opened.

2

GRAND DESIGNS

MENTION Carnegie Hall anywhere outside a 10-mile radius of Dunfermline and the chances are that whoever you're talking to will think of New York. Hardly surprisingly. Carnegie Hall is one of the world's great concert venues, standing at the Manhattan Island intersection it has graced since 1891. All the great names of music have performed there ... Caruso, Tchaikovsky, Ellington, Casals, Bernstein. US Presidents have spoken there. Even Mark Twain has addressed its vast tiers of seats. At one time it housed the American Academy of Dramatic Art, which boasted such pupils as Spencer Tracy, Anne Bancroft and Edward G. Robinson.

Sinatra's 'Live at Carnegie Hall' was recorded in its massive 3,000-seat auditorium on the corner of Seventh Avenue and Fifty-seventh Street — not in the prim-fronted and more modest 600-seater at the end of the Auld Grey Toun's East Port.

Yet... who knows what megastars might have put Dunfermline on their list of world venues if the original schemes for a concert hall had survived the arguments and back-biting of the Twenties and Thirties and taken its place as the Albert Hall of the north, slap bang in the middle of Pittencrieff Glen.

Every story must have a beginning. For Carnegie Hall it was the creation by the Carnegie Dunfermline Trust of a small school of music at Woodhead Street in 1905. Just a couple of years later it had become so successful that it moved to larger premises in the New Row and by the 1920s had some 600 pupils.

However this success did not please the Carnegie Trustees. They felt it was less a school of music than a building where music teachers could come along, get a room and equipment free of charge, and teach their own pupils. Nearly a third of these pupils didn't even come from Dunfermline!

What was wanted, declared the Trust, was a teaching staff more under their control, dedicated to encouraging talent wherever it was spotted and imparting to the school more a feeling of 'belonging'.

Allied to this encouragement of musical ability was a desire to 'foster and elevate the taste for music in the community' by way of concerts and lectures.

Remember that phrase. It was to crop up time and time again in the ensuing years as arguments raged over what should be the bill of fare for the good folk of Dunfermline.

At that time though, there was no doubt. Regular Saturday night concerts attracted huge audiences. St Margaret's Hall and Pilmuir Hall were favourite venues for these and other entertainments. In 1918 the Trustees acquired property at the junction of Bridge Street and Chalmers Street with a view to building their own concert hall. The expansion of music in the community must have been very much on their minds at the time because they also bought property at the corner of New Row and Park Avenue to develop a greatly expanded music school.

No less an architectural figure than George Washington Browne was called in. He had built the Edinburgh Central Library as a Carnegie gift more than 40 years earlier and had also been behind Glasgow City Chambers, the Royal Hospital for Sick Children in Edinburgh and many others. He came up with a 1,500-seat hall on the Bridge Street — Chalmers Street site, including an entrance directly on to the Glen, equally suitable for afternoon concerts or evening shows. Promenades were planned on three sides, making the place a virtual winter garden.

But the proposals aroused considerable opposition, a situation that was to arise time and time again during the next few years, with so many plans and counter plans that it's difficult now to determine exactly what was being proposed at any one time.

Some said the hall should be much bigger, others that it should be smaller, and there was criticism of its position within the Glen.

The Carnegie Trustees abandoned the project.

In 1923 as King George V, Queen Mary and the Duke and Duchess of York paid a royal visit to Dunfermline, the concert hall project raised its head again, with consideration being given to the possibility of buying and then totally refurbishing St Margaret's Hall, just beside the library on a site where now stands nothing more cultural than a car park.

Following a special report by Sir Walford Davies, Director of Music at the University of Wales, the emphasis at the School of Music was changed from elementary education in the subject to music as a recreational activity. It was kept a bit quiet though, the Dunfermline Press drawing readers' attentions to a reference to the premises 'hitherto known as the School of Music' and asked when exactly it had ceased to be so. They certainly didn't know about it.

No one may have told the great local public. Nevertheless the school disappeared — to be replaced by a Music Institute, still under the Director of Music, Mr David Stephen.

The Trust decided that full-scale alterations to St Margaret's Hall would be too costly and even if work had gone ahead there would still be room only for some 1,000, not nearly enough to house all those who would soon see the errors of their earlier ways and come flocking in.

By the end of 1924 the hunt was on again for a site ... a special reserve fund had been set up to finance the new hall. There was no doubt the place would be up and running soon.

But was it REALLY necessary? While they were claiming that St. Margaret's Hall could never be big enough, the Trustees were also bewailing the fact that they had not been receiving the local patronage they were 'entitled to expect' for musical activities.

In fact the whole project nearly bit the dust in 1928 when the £25,000 reserve fund was merged into a general fund and almost disappeared into the construction of a country home at Bandrum for ailing and convalescent children and the new Glen Gates in Chalmers Street. This happened several times as cases were made out for the more immediate need of such projects as the Glen Pavilion and the sports facilities at Pitreavie.

In 1928 Mrs Louise Carnegie came to Dunfermline to formally open the Andrew Carnegie Birthplace Memorial in Moodie Street, and townspeople were reminded of the great man's own words that the funds were left in trust 'dedicated for the purpose of providing the means of introducing into the daily lives of the masses such privileges and enjoyments as are under the present circumstances considered beyond their reach'.

Music had opened up for him a 'new and higher world' and he had decreed that his money should be used to 'bring into the monotonous lives of the toiling masses of Dunfermline more of sweetness and light'.

In New York in 1891 he'd built the Carnegie Music Hall, then put his hand into his pocket again and guaranteed an orchestra of '80 men, musicians good and true'. Now, more than 30 years later, a similar project in his home town led to one of the most confusing, and at times bitterest, periods in local history.

The 'Press' said at the time: 'When the full story of the Trustees' proposed new concert hall is written it should constitute a very curious document indeed'.

I don't know whether this book constitutes that curious document or not ... but events in 1928 were certainly very curious.

Even as the plans were agreed, the Convener of the Trust's Music Committee, Mr William Black, was hitting out at the lack of local music appreciation, and the Trustees went on to decide that no more celebrity or Scottish Orchestra concerts would be held due to poor attendances. This was the fault, according to some people, of the BBC, whose wireless shows were providing entertainment without anyone having to go outside on cold winter nights.

Others blamed hard seats in St Margaret's Hall. They didn't contribute much to the comfort of those who did make the effort of going out for their entertainment.

Live shows seemed to be on the way out nationwide ... yet a deputation was sent as far afield as Newcastle and Bournemouth to study their hall facilities.

So, as three Dunfermline schoolgirls cut the ribbons to officially open the new Louise Carnegie Gates in Chalmers Street, the original Washington Browne plans for a vast winter garden were being shelved and the architect was asked to submit, for a site north of this entrance, new plans for a building circular in shape and of a type that had caught the eye of the England touring party.

Confusion over the exact spot brought a flood of protest letters to the 'Press', many of them worried that the plans would entail moving the Carnegie Statue from a place he had himself approved — at the highest point in the Glen, against a natural background of tall trees, with the whole picture from the High Street direction enhanced by the new gates.

The Trustees, thundered the 'Press' leader column, were conducting the whole affair behind a 'shroud of secrecy'. It should be a matter for open discussion, especially as the statue wasn't the Trust's anyway but had been erected by public subscription.

William Black pointed out that Carnegie had said to erect 'needed structures on the margin of the Glen'. By moving the statue to the front of the new building the view would be improved not ruined.

Even the Trust was divided. Former Provost James Currie Macbeth who, a decade later, was to officially declare the new hall open, strongly opposed the site and was one of what seemed like hundreds who made their feeling known in the letters columns. Apart from him, though, letter writers didn't seem to have names in those days, signing themselves Harmonic Music, Subscriber, Pro Bono Publico and Critic No.1.

Out of the blue the Trustees abandoned both the statue site and the St. Margaret's Hall modernisation, which they'd been looking at yet again.

Suggested sites then included the Abbey Gardens Works, which later became the old bus station just up the hill from the Carnegie Museum, and even the Public Park, just the other side of what is now a dual carriageway from where the Carnegie Hall was eventually built. There it could 'crown the hill, near the flagstaff, as Benachie does a little to the west'. There was a lovely view from there and 'no one uses it except the cows'.

Sir JOHN ROSS. The man Carnegie himself chose to lead his Trust in 1903, he threatened to take his successors to court rather than allow them to build a hall within Pittencrieff Park.

All was quiet for about a year before, again out of the blue, the Trust announced that the years of argument were over. A hall and winter garden were definitely to be constructed on a site within the Glen, at the Pittencrieff Street entrance, opposite Maitland Street. Again it was planned by Washington Browne, now Sir George (and the first non-painter to be elected President of the Royal Scottish Academy).

ANDREW CARNEGIE'S statue in Pittencrieff Park, as seen from the High Street. It was this vista that critics of the hall-in-the-park plan thought would be lost for ever.

It would cost £60,000 and seat 1,500 plus another 300 standing when sliding glass partitions into the promenade areas were opened.

The decision was reached by a majority 12-10 vote, Life Trustees going against it but being outvoted by the Councillors on the Board of Trustees.

The proposed building was immediately attacked as being too far removed from the town centre and described as 'a disappointing malformation of a mongrel building, erected on a wretched hole of a site'.

Not much room for doubt about that citizen's feelings! Nor was there about those of Sir John Ross, the man Carnegie had chosen to lead his Trust and who had retired as Chairman in 1923.

He described it as the most inconvenient site in all Dunfermline, a weary walk for most and impossible for those in Rosyth, Brucefield, and Townhill. St. Margaret's Hall had to be the choice. With new seats, lights and heating it would be more than adequate for a town whose people would not be cajoled or scolded into attending concerts. There was no doubt in his mind that it could be done very cheaply.

Some supported the Glen site, pointing out that there were tramways available to get the people there. Others looked ahead to when the Glen Bridge was completed, allowing access to the model lodging house inhabitants from the Bruce Street area. For them, the winter gardens could make a first-class doss-house!

In another 'shroud of secrecy' the plan was scrapped and, unbelievably, they started looking again at the infamous statue site. Like a clap of thunder, Sir John Ross, writing from Grantown-on-Spey, said the Trustees were acting counter to the Trust Deed and he personally would bring legal action to stop proceedings! Shortly after his 94th birthday, Sir John confirmed to the then Chairman of Trustees, James Norval, that he would interdict the Trust — not knowing that the site had already been rejected once again.

A few weeks later Sir John Ross died.

William Black, the Music Committee Convener, admitted that his colleagues did not see eye to eye with him and declared himself 'beaten but not dismayed'. Shortly afterwards he was announcing a Music Institute and concert practice hall to compare with anything in Britain.

The first step towards this came when they bought Benachie, the big house at the end of the East Port, from the late Sir William Robertson's estate.

Sir William, Lord Lieutenant of Fife, had been a member of the Trust since the beginning. As Vice-Chairman at the time of Sir John Ross's retiral, he had been expected to take up the reins, but died just a few days before the meeting at which he would have become Chairman.

Mr James Moodie was appointed part-time Director of Music and in 1933 details were announced of exactly what the new practice hall would be like. It was to be built on the west side of Benachie, linked by corridor to the Institute, and would seat either 400 or 600, the figure to be decided later.

There would be no going back. The grand designs for the Glen were torn up and the special reserve cash fund closed.

The 'Press' heading that weekend put it bluntly enough: 'Concert Hall Abandoned'.

It seems, certainly now, a rather odd headline. True, there would be no grandiose structure accommodating 1,800. But what Dunfermline was to get was still a concert hall — one perhaps more realistic in scale, and certainly of fine quality. And for the Glen, the Trustees were simultaneously announcing plans for a shelter and band auditorium, another 600-seater hall which would become the Music Pavilion.

THE lands of Benachie originally stretched from the East Port all the way down to where the railway station now stands, and were owned by one John Liddell of London. Eventually most of it was sold to the town council and became the Public Park, but parts of it to the north were leased out. What is now the Music Institute was acquired by Andrew Wallace, a coalmaster, who named it Hawthornbank. The land slightly to the east was leased by Bailie Steedman, the Postmaster, and was called Brierlyhill.

When Steedman died, his house was taken over by the Wallace family who eventually knocked it down and added an extension to Hawthornbank, as well as building, in 1900, the little lodge house which stood at the top of what is now the new road through the park.

In 1909, the house was bought by the Robertson family, who changed the name to Benachie. They owned it until it was sold to Carnegie Dunfermline Trust in 1933 for the new Music Institute.

The Robertson initials can still be seen carved into an ornate fireplace in a corridor of the Music Institute.

14

THE little lodge house which was built along with the extension to Benachie in 1900 stood at the original entrance to the Institute and Hall until it was demolished in 1970. Now, on that site, the new road through the public park opens out on to Sinclair Gardens roundabout at the end of the East Port.

THE Carnegie Music Institute as it looked in 1968, owned by the Council, still then run by the Trust.

3

OPEN FOR BUSINESS

AFTER the years of wrangling over a concert hall for Dunfermline, opening day was almost an anti-climax. The protagonists joined together in welcoming the new place, whether it was exactly what they had wanted or not. Peace and harmony reigned ... for a little while at least.

Mrs Carnegie had been invited to perform the opening but advancing years and ill-health kept her in America. While in Scotland to receive the Freedom of Edinburgh, she had, however, managed to visit the site and inspect progress on the Hall's construction.

Acute labour shortages and Government requirements, with one eye on the worsening situation in Europe, made it difficult to obtain all the materials as they were needed, but by the Spring of 1937 the hall was well nigh completed and an official opening date was set for October 6th.

Yet even on that grand day things weren't completely ready. Guests attending the glittering occasion had to negotiate temporary steps and wind their way through piles of building rubble before they could enter the luxurious new concert hall.

Rubble apart, the exterior had a look of quality. Built entirely of stone from the Darney Quarries in Northumberland, it had the classic look of a hall made to house chamber concerts. Features of the front include 'fluted pillars with chastely carved capitals' and accommodation was provided for 640 — 220 of them in the gallery directly above the main entrance.

Specially adapted plaster was inserted at certain parts of the interior to ensure as perfect acoustics as could be achieved. Two spacious foyers, one upstairs and one down, were linked by staircases on either side of the main entrance. Walls throughout were panelled to a height of about seven feet.

At the side of each foyer were toilet suites. The whole auditorium, upstairs and down, was fitted with the latest in tip-up chairs, the electric lighting neatly concealed. Ventilation came from hidden skylights along the roof.

It ranked as one of the best-equipped halls in Scotland, with the very latest in stage lighting. It also had space set aside for the provision of an organ although this was never completed.

After so many years of to-ing and fro-ing and bringing in the big guns of Scottish architecture, ironically the place was eventually built to a design by the local firm of Muirhead & Rutherford. Glaziers were the small local firm of C.R. Smith — now one of Britain's giant double-glazing concerns.

The place was built to last. In 1986 some of the panelling at the back of the auditorium was removed to make way for a new control box and inside were found the signatures of some of the joiners who installed it. They were recognised by Dunfermline man Jim Gardner, who was a 14-year-old apprentice at that time.

He thought it an outstanding design but for him it meant a lot of hard work. The stairs were made of pitch pine, notable for its hardness. A couple of strokes with a plane and you had to stop to clean off the resin and sharpen it again.

He worked for Anderson & Pert and the shaping of the treads was done at their yard in Woodmill Street, almost under the railway viaduct.

But, tough as the work was, the finished job is such that the staircase would probably still be standing if the rest of the place fell down around it!

Back in 1937 the invited guests tramped through the new foyer and up those stairs that would last forever to look down on a stage decorated with ferns and scarlet geraniums.

THE FIRST recital in Carnegie Hall was by American pianist Webster Aitken.

EARLY performers at Carnegie Hall were the Lener String Quartet.

Presiding over the opening ceremony, the Convener of the Music Committee, William Black, declared himself delighted with the new hall, even though it was perhaps a little less than he had hoped for. 'In providing and equipping such a suite of buildings as this', he continued, 'it is not the object of the Trust to produce musical experts or even professional musicians. Their aim is rather the development of amateur talent, the practice and display of which yields so much pleasure and adds so much to our communal life.

'Don't get away with the idea that because this has been called a Chamber Concert Hall, it is to be entirely devoted to the production of Chamber Music which, in some minds, can be enjoyed only by the highbrows. It is for the development of music of every kind.'

The Trust Chairman, James Currie Macbeth, described the Hall as a luxury which should appeal to the cultural side of the community.

Once when he had spoken to Andrew Carnegie in Pittsburgh, Carnegie had said: 'When you build a hall, do not make the mistake of making it too large.' That was the only direction, said Mr Macbeth, he ever heard Carnegie make in regard to the administration of the Trust.

'This hall, from now onwards, shall be known as the Carnegie Hall and I declare the hall open. I trust that the citizens of Dunfermline will take a personal and individual interest in it.'

After a prayer of dedication by the Rev. William Andrew Hutchison, singer Broomfield Robertson performed an ancient Celtic dedication arranged by James Moodie, and a small choir sang 'Except the Lord Build the House', a motet repeated later that evening by a full choir of 80 during the Hall's opening concert.

The Dunfermline Press, in its leader column, also made a direct plea to local people to use the place. 'It rests with the citizens,' it said, 'especially the younger generation, to make full use of the splendid new opportunities placed at their disposal'.

And the Hall certainly got into its stride quickly, with performances of operas by the Music Institute company and the first Chamber Concert of the season — the first ever in Carnegie

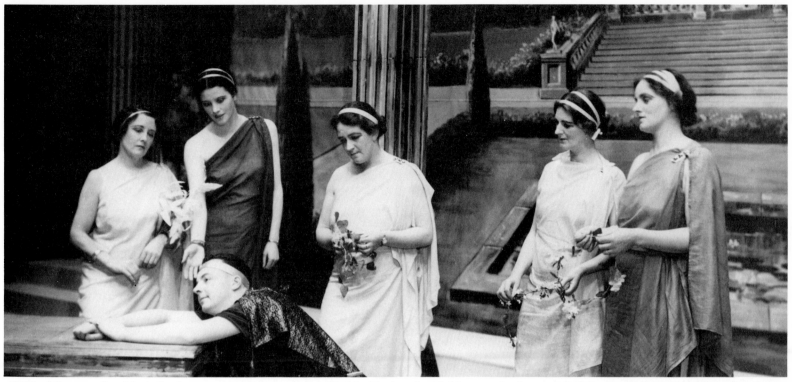

ONE of the very first Music Institute operas performed was Gluck's 'Orpheus' and this scene is photographed 'at the tomb of Euridice', with Enid Wilson, Stephanie Carty, Helen Drysdale (also Institute superintendent), Mrs Craig and Mrs Weir along with David Scott as Orpheus.

Hall — took place a few days later with a recital by the brilliant American pianist, Webster Aitken.

Aitken put on a special afternoon show first especially for youngsters, at which Moodie introduced the pianist and W. Prentice Torrance gave explanatory notes on the pieces as they went along.

Other first-year Chamber Concerts came from the Philharmonic Ensemble Trio, Flora Collins and John Simons, the Boyd Neel String Orchestra, the Lener String Quartet and Mark Raphael, among others.

Then Mr Macbeth put his foot in it. Addressing Dunfermline Rotary Club, he disagreed with James Moodie's belief that everyone's level of musical appreciation should be virtually forced on to a high plane. He personally detested jazz and crooning but ultra-classical music too was beyond his enjoyment.

Asked to enlarge on the theme by the 'Press', he said that he could not agree to spend Trust cash on comparatively few enthusiasts: he had to cater for the majority, the common people. Even the most eminent of artists sometimes could barely half-fill the Hall.

AMONG the well-known performers during the first few months of Carnegie Hall concerts were the Boyd Neel Orchestra.

It evoked a storm of protests: some angrily pointed out that the appreciation of highbrow was not confined to the upper class, and that many 'workers' enjoyed it just as much. Others worried that Macbeth's personal preferences would in future cloud the issue of what would be performed, although the Editor apologised the following week for such an accusation being printed.

Others simply pointed to the empty seats at these concerts and said Macbeth was putting into words what most people were thinking.

War had broken out within the pages of the 'Press' ... and elsewhere, as it turned out. A few hundred miles to the east Hitler invaded Poland and plunged the world into turmoil. The Poles came to have a particular importance for Dunfermline as Carnegie Hall suspended its little local skirmishes and went to war for real.

William Black
Convener, Carnegie
Dunfermline Trust
Music Committee

James Currie Macbeth
Chairman,
Carnegie Dunfermline Trust

4

WAR FOOTING

IN October 1939 the Battle of Britain was still in the future: newspapers talked of the Phoney War, the period when there were official hostilities with Germany but nothing nasty seemed to be happening.

But that was in London. In the Forth Valley, the war was real. Watchers on the seafront at Kirkcaldy saw Spitfires hound and harass a Junkers 88 until it dived into the water, pouring smoke, the RAF's first kill of the war.

A few miles to the west the Carnegie Dunfermline Trustees were putting all their buildings at the disposal of the authorities, to be used as barracks, first aid posts, hospitals.

Ironic in a way that men of war should be accommodated in places which owed their existence to a man who had spent 1½ million dollars on building the Peace Palace in The Hague.

Director of Music James Moodie suggested that the Institute become a centre for locally-based servicemen and it was handed over to the YMCA for use as a social club and canteen. It remained open as such until some eight weeks after peace was declared six years later.

Moodie himself took charge, helped by the superintendent, Miss Helen Drysdale, and they put in a vast number of hours there on a voluntary basis. There was a small kitchen staff but all the rest of the help came from groups of women from local churches, guilds and the like.

Overnight the practice rooms became dining rooms, reading and writing rooms, lounges, games rooms catering for billiards, darts and table tennis. Quickly it was realised that even Benachie wasn't big enough for the task and a temporary extension was built of timber, standing on brick piers, to the east of the main building. It would be used as additional canteen facilities.

The Annexe, as it was known, turned out to be a bit less temporary than envisaged. Long after the war ended it was bought by the Council and remained in existence until the mid-1980s, when it was demolished to make way for the permanent small hall annexe which now stands on the same spot.

Light meals of tea, coffee and sandwiches were always available, especially in the mornings, while more substantial plates of sausages and chips and the like made their appearance in the evenings. A mobile canteen service went out to gun posts and balloon barrage units, dispensing food, cigarettes, books, etc.

A gramophone room was extremely popular and the Annexe, when not in use as a canteen, doubled as a centre for social gatherings. In all, perhaps some 50,000 servicemen at one time or another attended the Saturday night dances held there to music provided by 'Mr McKissock and his radio apparatus'. On Sundays there were church services.

Local concert parties entertained there, as well as history lectures and art shows and — just the thing to give the troops — Ministry of Information lectures. Gracie Fields sang to the sailors at Rosyth but didn't quite make it up the hill to the town. After its first year in operation, it received the accolade of a royal visit from the Duchess of Gloucester.

It was estimated that perhaps a million services personnel could have crossed the threshold of the Institute during its war years, and at the end of hostilities the front door steps were so worn that they had to be filled in and relevelled!

Carnegie Hall joined in the effort when its use was offered free for Forces entertainment. As the Services Theatre it brought light relief to the lives of some 50,000 people and became a popular Sunday evening rendezvous. Again local talent put on the early shows, later augmented by official ENSA parties.

WARTIME comforts for the servicemen who used Carnegie Hall and the Music Institute, with James Moodie (left) giving a helping hand.

MARIAN NOWAKOWSKI. a top Polish bass who was billeted in Dunfermline during the war and later returned to give many Carnegie Hall performances.

For many people in the Thirties and Forties James Moodie WAS the Music Institute. Although officially its **part-time** Director of Music, he seemed to be there day and night. He was a kindly but strict teacher, with a little white West Highland Terrier which sat on thick cushions in an alcove of the rooom while he was teaching.

There seemed to be nothing in his life but music. When he wasn't teaching, he was writing, composing or conducting.

When he did get away from the Institute, he lived in a succession of cheap lodgings, seemingly never putting down real roots.

He was a native of Dumfries, where he was playing the organ at the age of 15. When he moved to Fife he became organist at Carnock, then in 1933 was appointed Director of Music at the Institute when it moved to Benachie. He was also Abbey organist and Master of Song in Dunfermline as well as being appointed conductor of the Royal Choral Union in Edinburgh.

Throughout his life in Dunfermline he was constantly involved in disagreements over his avowed policy of educating the masses to appreciate a better class of music ... even if that was the last thing they wanted!

He eventually retired in 1956, giving up all his musical titles and posts. By February the following year he was dead.

Among the top performers of the war years were the Polish Army Choir. Many Poles were billeted in Fife and their concerts were a treat not to be missed.

One of the soloists was a lieutenant with a magnificent but untrained voice, Marian Nowakowski, who went on to find fame as one of the world's great basses. At the Music Institute he was delighted to get singing lessons from Moodie, the two communicating in mutually bad French until the Pole picked up some English, spoken in a broad Fife accent!

Moodie made an arrangement of 'Annie Laurie' for Nowakowski, with which he delighted audiences all over the world, always telling the story of how he came by the song. Another Scottish song recorded by him, the 'Eriskay Love Lilt', was one of ten favourites chosen by the then Princess Elizabeth at Christmas 1947.

As thanks for all the kindness shown to the Poles by local people, one of their number, Lieutenant Mieczkowski, executed a fine commemorative painting on the wall of the Music Institute lounge and this can still be seen in the Institute today.

It wasn't only the Polish Army, ENSA and Saturday night dances during the war years, however. Much of the teaching work simply moved from the Institute to the Hall, where every available inch of space, in cupboards, corridors and foyers, was utilised. If the sirens went everyone was supposed to dive under the stage.

Top-class concerts were still taking place, of course. Glasgow-born Frederick Lamond, one of the world's great pianists, gave a recital there at the age of 74: Moura Lympany was soloist with the London Philharmonic: Benno Moiseiwitch was there in 1942. Rawicz and Landauer appeared before a capacity audience and tickets for a recital by Dame Myra Hess had all gone within hours of going on sale. For her they even put extra seats on to the side of the stage to take care of some of the overflow.

The Glasgow Orpheus Choir sold out and attendances generally were immensely encouraging, despite the limitations of the blackout.

A Dane, S. Beyer-Pedersen, gave a talk on what it was like to have your own home and country occupied by enemy forces ... and suddenly it was all over. Peace came back into everyone's lives.

Free use of the facilities was discontinued ... and there came the shock news that the Trust's income wasn't enough now to support many activities on their pre-war scale. Proposals would be laid before the Town Council that they take over certain activities to be run as social amenities. The actual existence of many of these was threatened.

Townspeople, brought up to think of the Carnegie purse as bottomless, thought this was some sort of bluff, aimed perhaps at getting a contribution towards the running of these facilities. It wouldn't really happen, they scoffed.

But in July, 1945 came the transfer of the Baths, Gymnasium, District Institutes and Bandrum Home, followed soon afterwards by the bowling greens.

The war had changed many things; it was about to change the face of Dunfermline.

JACK WRIGHT was just nine years old when he first went to live in Benachie Lodge, the little cottage next door to what is now the Music Institute. His father, Thomas, was gardener to Sir William Robertson, and when the Trust took over he remained there, becoming caretaker of the Institute and later the Hall. Jack and his young wife, Elizabeth, moved to Bolton where he worked as an engineer, but when his father retired in 1947 he came home to take over.

In fact it turned out to be more than just a job ... their lives were devoted to the place and the standards of cleanliness were legend. The Nolan Sisters once left a note of thanks for 'the cleanest theatre they'd every played' and one amateur company, needing to dirty some clothes to give a scruffy appearance, eventually had someone climb one of the outside lights to get a good bit of honest dirt from the top of the globe. Every corner inside was spotless!

They got involved in the shows, Jack with a team of helpers working the lights and shifting the scenery, and Lizzie helping out with props. Cups of tea were made at all sorts of time for 'really nice people' like Robert Wilson, Peter Morrison, Robin Hall and Jimmie McGregor, and the Corries. The latter were in the theatre when Jack retired and were invited along to his party.

When Jack's mother was seriously ill, the Polish bass, Marian Nowakowski, who had been based in Dunfermline during the war and sung at Carnegie Hall many times, came down to the Lodge specially to see her.

The Lodge was knocked down in 1970 to make way for the new roundabout and the Wrights moved to a house a few hundred yards away. But even after he retired in 1976, Jack continued to help the new caretaker, Bobby Nicholson, whenever he could. Even when he died in 1981, it still wasn't the end of his connection with the place.

He had jokingly promised Bobby: 'I'll come back and haunt you!' And years later Bobby, finding lights on he was certain he had switched off the night before, would tell Lizzie Wright; 'Jack was in the Hall last night'.

JACK and Elizabeth Wright at Carnegie Hall ... along with the Institute, their workplace and virtual home for most of their married life.

JACK with The Corries, guests at his retiral party.

5

A HOSTILE PEACE

THE INK had barely dried on the peace treaties before James Moodie re-opened hostilities on the home front. Now Director of Music to the Carnegie Dunfermline Trust, Abbey organist, Master of the Song in Dunfermline, and conductor of the Royal Choral Union in Edinburgh, his first warning shots came in a three-part series written for the 'Dunfermline Press' entitled 'What's the use of music anyway?' It was a thinly disguised plea for the people to take time to learn how to appreciate classical music — and a plea for more cash to help this along.

Then, as he met a storm of protest over his snobbish attitude, he opened up with the big guns. He submitted to the Trust a document outlining what their post-war policy should be.

'The object is the widening and deepening of musical appreciation and experience, to the end that music may become more and more an integral part of the life of the community and an important factor in its cultural and spiritual development. Nothing less should be envisaged.'

And just in case there had ever been any doubt about how deeply he felt this, he concluded: 'To regard music as **mere entertainment** is to miss entirely its true mission and underestimate its value.'

Strong words: he was out to educate the people whether they wanted educating or not.

Unfortunately it seemed not. A report commissioned by the Trust concluded that only on rare occasions was seating capacity fully taken up: often only a few dozen enthusiasts were there.

There was a claim by some that the place did not have the atmosphere of a real theatre: others said it was too far from the town centre, and most of those interviewed thought it a place only for those with a leaning towards the highbrow. The report made the point that on occasion 'private enterprise has brought artistes of no greater eminence, yet Carnegie Hall has been filled to overflowing. In some cases admission was double that charged for Trust entertainments'.

Some thirty years later a survey conducted by the Friends of Carnegie Hall showed that local attitudes towards the place had hardly changed at all.

The calibre of guest artist then was indeed high, with performances by Leon Goossens, Kathleen Ferrier, Joan Hammond, violinist Albert Sammons, and a Theatre Workshop produced under the eagle eye of Joan Littlewood.

Tom Allan, now aged 78 and the hall's official fireman since 1940, recalls Sir Harry Lauder doing a concert for the Firemen's Benevolent Fund in 1946 ... and the mean Scot belied his reputation by doing it for nothing. All he asked was that someone drive down to his home at Lauder Hall in the Borders to pick him up, feed him after the show, then take him home again.

There were financial successes but when even Dunfermline man Ian Whyte conducting the BBC Scottish Orchestra could only half fill the Hall, Moodie's dream began to turn into a nightmare ... at least financially. The Boyd Neel Orchestra, a top-class outfit who had been one of the Hall's earliest successes, could by the early 1950s attract only a couple of hundred patrons ... and a loss of £120. A Founder's Day concert featuring Ian Wallace lost even more.

One near full house listened while the BBC broadcast from the Hall an edition of 'A Matter of Opinion'. Chaired by the author Neil Paterson, the panel consisted of MP Alexander Anderson, Councillor Miss Betty Harvie Anderson, farmer John Fowlie, and 'News Chronicle' diarist Ian Mackay.

Producer George Runcie told the countrywide radio listeners that he was speaking from a beautiful hall which could not be surpassed throughout the length and breadth of Scotland.

But what the professionals and celebrities were failing to do, the amateurs managed ... night after night. Dunfermline Light Opera Club filled the hall for 12 nights with 'The Desert Song,' and put £400 surplus into the coffers of local charities. Kelty sold out for two weeks with 'Showboat', and some of the amateur companies fitted in extra matinees and even a third Monday if the Hall wasn't booked by someone else. Even the Boy Scouts were a sell-out.

Between 1947 and 1963 Dunfermline man Jimmy Hunter put on 11 Gang Shows, his 230 performers on stage at the one time making it Britain's biggest, and he set off this very professional amateur show with a full 18-piece orchestra.

Hunter had been a drummer with Nat Gonella and his Georgians, one of the country's leading popular bands, which boasted at one time Mantovani as its guitarist. He was also a lifelong supporter of the Scout movement.

When he first became involved in producing a show for local Scouts, he went to see the originator of the Gang Show, Ralph Reader, and they swapped ideas. Hunter came away with many of the Reader scripts, then set about rewriting them for a Scottish audience. The show became so big eventually that another entertainment was booked for the Annexe to keep the younger boys happy while they waited their turn to go on to the big stage!

One memorable performance from that period saw 70 Scouts, the 'men' in tuxedos, the 'women' in black-and-white dresses, criss-crossing the stage singing 'Strolling', the front dozen with six black and six white poodles.

Like many of the amateur shows at the time, so successful did they become that queues used to form at Muir's Music Shop on the day tickets went on sale. For the Scouts, the proceeds of this success bought for them Nineacres camp site at Crook of Devon.

Jimmy Hunter's connections with Carnegie Hall have lasted 40 years. He put on many shows himself, using both amateur and professional performers, produced the Provost's Command show for ten years, and acted as compere for shows involving Andy Stewart, John Cairney, the Bachelors, and dozens more.

But as he made his Carnegie debut, others involved in the Hall's story were disappearing. Mrs Louise Carnegie died, preceding by just a few weeks the man who had fought so hard and long for a concert hall, the Music Convener, William Black. There was a farewell concert by students of the College of Hygiene, before they headed North to their new home in Aberdeen (from where they later moved to Cramond, still as Dunfermline College of Physical Education).

James Currie Macbeth, the man who performed the official opening ceremony, died at the age of 89, and James Moodie, who had devoted his life to trying to make Dunfermline's citizens more musically cultured, retired.

The Institute and the Hall had been Moodie's life and, in a very short time, the musician who started his career as organist at Carnock Parish Church was dead.

For the Trust it was a time of financial stringency. Retirals weren't replaced, teachers were asked to double what they paid for hiring a room, from one shilling to two, and the Institute opened at 2 p.m. instead of 9.30 a.m. In the Hall shows still lost money and the Trust decided not to put on any more concerts themselves.

Even before the Provost's Command Shows there was a regular event to round off Civic Week, a jamboree of happenings scattered all over the town which had started as an annual event in 1948.

There were dancing displays and Gilbert & Sullivan, often by the Queen Anne School drama group, dramas, children's shows, choirs, dog training, gymnastics ... most of it featuring local people although there were appearances by Robert Wilson, Johnnie Beattie and once a Top of the Town talent show hosted by Archie McCulloch, who did that very same thing for radio.

In the second Civic Week there was a prize of £5. 5/- to be won for a song about Dunfermline. The winner was the Rev. A. Penman, from Ontario, Canada, no less, and his 'Auld Grey Toun' was set to music by James Moodie.

The Hall began to spread its wings to attract customers. A magicians' conference came to town and two members of the successful 1953 Everest expedition brought along a lecture and slide show. There was a full house in the evening and an even more enthusiastic gathering in the afternoon of pupils from the town's schools.

That show made national headlines when it was reported that four Queen Anne boys had been refused the chance to go because they were not wearing school uniform. This was denied by County Council Education officials but parents stuck to their story and the row rumbled on.

Another capacity crowd saw a concert by Soviet performers, including the Bolshoi's baritone, Eugen Belov, who sang 'The Bonnie Banks' in a fine Doric accent.

One of the biggest productions at the Hall was 'The Masque of Dunfermline' in 1957. A 'live history' of the town, it featured many local choirs, drama groups and music societies, starting off with the marriage of Princess Margaret and Malcolm Canmore, and also depicted events such as Edward, the Hammer of the Scots, ordering the Monastery of Dunfermline to be pulled down as it was a stronghold of rebellion.

Among the English hordes taking the stage 'Dunfermline' apart were not a few real Englishmen, from the Services and the Dockyard, who set about their task with a rare will!

One major scene depicted the great fire of 1624, which destroyed half the town ... just as the great fire of 1957 nearly destroyed the Masque. It happened in Edinburgh, gutting the premises of theatrical costumiers Mutrie's, who were supplying most of the costumes for the show.

Other groups, museums, and all sorts of people nationwide rallied round and, although some costumes weren't eventually 100 per cent accurate for their period, enough were made available to let the show go ahead after a last-minute scramble. One very genuine costume was used in the show: the uniform worn by the 'Earl of Elgin' was the actual outfit worn by the real Earl of that period, loaned by the current Earl when he heard about the disaster.

The show was rescued ... what no one knew at that time was that very soon it would be the Hall itself which would be looking for a rescuer.

WHO'S this likely-looking lad then? Nelson Eddy perhaps, singing his heart out to Rose Marie? Not quite ... in fact the 'Mountie' outfit is the uniform of the Royal Corps of Signals Band, and this was their baritone soloist when they played Carnegie Hall in 1954. He was, according to a newspaper critic at the time, someone who, 'when a few years have passed over his head, ought to become a baritone to reckon with'.

National Serviceman Hill certainly did just that. As Vince Hill he became one of the country's best-known popular singers. But in 1954 he was singing songs from The Barber of Seville, and, with truncheons borrowed from the local nick, 'The Gendarmes' with another lad who 'got on', Martin Taylor, helped at the piano by the brilliant Keith Swallow.

SIR Harry Lauder, the 'mean Scot' who took part in a Carnegie Hall show in aid of firemen's charities ... for transport to and from the hall and a good free meal.

THE FAMOUS
VICTORY VERSATILES
IN
"HAPPY DAZE"
(First Edition)
WITH
SIR HARRY LAUDER

6

FOR SALE

By the early Sixties things looked good for the Hall. It catered for a much wider range of events. The SWRI held their annual conference there, the RSPB put on birdlife films ... people were beginning to use the place.

The Music Institute too was being used to the limit of its space and time. As well as all the classes held there, it had achieved worldwide status for its resources, particularly its magnificent Music Library. There were music scores there that could be found nowhere else in the world.

It had been the first musical training ground for well-known conductors such as Ian Whyte and Kemlo Stephen, a son of its first Director. The wooden annexe, built to house wartime soldiers, was bought by the Trust for £250 and fitted with a small stage, so great was the demand for teaching and practice space.

Another huge Masque production was put on ... a drama festival adjudicator found the stage 'too wide' ... and the Hall's predecessor as Dunfermline's centre of high-class music and drama, St. Margaret's Hall, was gutted by fire, a desperate battle by firemen managing to save, almost untouched, the adjoining library, the first of over 2,800 world-wide provided by Andrew Carnegie.

Bertha Waddell was still a regular visitor ... and if you have to ask who she was, then you didn't go to school in Dunfermline. From 1932 until she retired in 1969 her Children's Theatre was a day out of class for the town's pupils as they got what, for many, was their first taste of live theatre.

But as a Carnegie Hall audience one night stood in shocked silence after hearing of the killing of John F. Kennedy, two other threats were creeping up unseen to do their bit towards finishing off live theatre ... television, and the Beatles.

In 1959 Polish bass Marian Nowakowski, guest soloist at the Dunfermline Orchestral Society's annual concert, had told a packed house. 'There is not one concert I sing at where I do not say a few words about this town and the joyous days I spent here.'

Four years later he played to less than 200 ... it was Z-cars on the telly that night and the nation were all viewing.

If they weren't, then the chances were that they were teenagers, practising the three chords they reckoned would be enough to take them and their guitars to fame and fortune. In the wake of the Fab Four's success, the nation sprouted some 17,000 instant beat groups, with an estimated £28 million being borrowed to buy new electrical instruments.

'In-home entertainment' for the older generation and the new pop culture of the youngsters were certainly insidious threats to the Hall's activities. Early in the 1960s the Trustees dropped a bombshell of their own.

For some years they had owned most of the properties east of Viewfield Terrace — an almost complete chain stretching from the Music Institute, Carnegie Hall, Tower House, the former Erskine Manse and the Dunfermline Museum to the Viewfield House Craft School. Once the Trustees had hoped to develop the whole site for an Arts complex. Now this dream was abandoned. Further, hit by rising costs, the Trustees' income was fully committed on existing schemes. If they wanted to pioneer anything new, they had to save over £10,000 a year — by shedding a number of existing activities.

So they began negotiations with the County Council about a possible takeover of Pitreavie Playing Fields, the Pilmuir Street Youth Centre and the Craft School: at the same time, aware of the Town Council's thoughts of a new Civic Centre, they opened negotiations for the transfer of the Hall and Institute, Tower House, the Erskine Manse, and the Dunfermline Museum.

Ultimately, after a couple of years of proposal and counter proposal, misunderstandings and clarifications, a deal was

THE Hall has its Tiffany Window ... the Institute has its hidden treasure in the shape of an ornate Victorian bathroom, complete with dark oak panels and shiny brass fittings on the magnificent bath/shower.

It was built in 1920 by the Robertson family who then owned the house, in anticipation of a visit by Ramsay MacDonald.

However, he was recalled to Parliament before his visit to Dunfermline, and the bathroom remains as a museum piece. But only just, for several times tourists have made instant offers to buy it and have it shipped to America.

hammered out. The Carnegie Hall was valued at £25,000 — but it would go to the Council free provided it continued to be used as a public hall and theatre. Similarly, the Dunfermline Museum would be conveyed as a free gift, again provided the building continued to be used as a museum. The Music Institute, Tower House, old Erskine Manse and the Craft School (unwanted by the County Council) would be sold for £25,000 with the Trust leasing back the Institute to be run just as before.

The Dunfermline Press carried pictures of all these properties under the headline 'The Crumbling Empire of the Carnegie Trust'. One national newspaper even told an open-mouthed world that little Dunfermline Town Council was about to take over the running of mighty Carnegie Hall ... in New York! Even 'The Times' devoted column inches to the news and suggested that, after a quarter of a million pounds had been spent on music and drama, and £3,000,000 on its citizens, Dunfermline people weren't grateful enough actually to use all the gifts available to them. Perhaps people were just unaware of how much of what they took for granted was funded by Carnegie money and not paid for from the rates.

Whatever the truth, Carnegie Hall now became a Town Council building...

7

TARTAN TRIUMPH

The Sixties and Seventies were the Swinging Years of British music ... but somebody forgot to mention them to Carnegie Hall. Pop fans marked the place down as highbrow and strictly for 'squares'. They failed in their hundreds to support shows when an apparently 'with it' management eventually got round to featuring some of the big names of the day.

The new owners of the Hall, the local Council, appointed a Halls and Entertainment Manager, Colin Reed, who looked on the place as belonging to the people, constantly in use for the community, with professional shows of all kinds being staged. Every age group and interest would be catered for.

Reed experimented with just about every conceivable package of entertainment, as did his successor, Lorraine Miller, and as the current manager, Jim McIsaac, is doing.

David Whitfield powered on to the stage with a superb act ... played to a handful of an audience. The Smurfs and Presto the Magic Rabbit put on wonderful children's shows, but there wasn't enough of the right sort of publicity around the town to pack them in. There was, however, excellent publicity, and some of the most exciting posters ever, for a Champagne Spectacular, a brilliant show that moved along quickly from beginning to end and was full of gorgeous Bluebell-type dancers ... but nobody came to that either!

Pop groups were obviously the in thing and in 1975 the flags were waved and the Council sat back smugly. The breakthrough had come. Showaddywaddy sold out: the youngsters were coming to Carnegie Hall, and they weren't looking at the place as just for highbrows any more.

But even in success there were problems. The new level of 'megastars' also asked 'mega' fees and a complete sell-out could cost the Council a loss of hundreds of pounds.

Within a few months the bubble had burst ... the Glitter Band show was cancelled, Alvin Stardust performed to a couple of hundred fans, and The Swinging Blue Jeans sold £26 worth of tickets. In May 1976 the Council decided: no more subsidised pop shows.

A survey revealed that out of some 70 shows on the Carnegie Hall stage that year, only seven made a profit, and they were all 'Scottish'. The White Heather Club, Andy Stewart, Lex McLean, The Corries, Callum Kennedy, Sydney Devine ... that was the stuff to give the troops, and swell the coffers.

Dunfermline producer and compere Jimmy Hunter, who had scored such a huge success with the Gang Shows, put on others like A Touch of Class and A Taste of Scotch, using local performers. He compered Kathy Kay, well-known at the time because of her weekly TV slot with the Billy Cotton Band Show.

And Sydney Devine came to town. The powers-that-be had barely heard of the man, yet he sold every ticket — and had the 40 and 50-year-old ladies literally screaming for more. A few years later The Platters, not the originals but in fact younger relatives of the singing group, had the same effect, with long queues of fans not quite still in their teens, patiently waiting for autographs and signed photos!

There was even a miniature circus on stage, complete with tent, ring, ponies, performing dogs ... the lot.

Derek Batey brought Mr & Mrs to town, and Opera House memories took a trick, with Bert Shorthouse, Billy Crockett (the brother of Dave Willis), and Ronnie Parnell among those playing the parts of old-time greats who had performed in the Dunfermline Opera House Variety Shows.

Former Bluebell Girl Audrey Mortimer's young dancers took part in these and in pantomime every Christmas. The Bachelors went down well, as did a rare treat for lovers of the big band sound: the band of the US Air Forces in Europe, the Ambassadors, direct from their base at Glen Miller Hall, Hamburg, and the descendants of the great man's own orchestra. They came for no fee, just free 'digs' in local homes and meals for the 19 bandsmen.

Hunter compered this and seemed to have his finger on the pulse of what would sell in Dunfermline. For ten years he also produced the Provost's Command Performance, the big show which ended every year's Civic Week and which has just been revived after a long gap.

Something else which had a ten-year lifespan during this period was the Carnegie Festival of Music and the Arts.

The heart of the Festival was a Symphony Orchestra, founded seven years earlier in Cumberland by the Director of Music at St. Bees School, Donald Leggat. When it was about to be discontinued there, the Carnegie Trust took it over and moved it lock, stock and barrel to Dunfermline. Sir John Barbirolli agreed to become President, and Leggat, its Conductor and Artistic Director, declared himself delighted with the facilities he found in Dunfermline. The first year had a varied menu in addition to the Orchestra's concerts. There was folk music from Archie Fisher, The Islanders, Dolina Maclennan and The Tregullion; dance from the Edinburgh Ballet Theatre and a late-night revue. Elsewhere there were chamber concerts and exhibitions.

The orchestra were students of music from the various colleges throughout Britain and Northern Ireland, working through their Easter vacation to gain experience playing in a large group. It was all organised by Fred Mann, the Trust Secretary, and he and the staff at the Trust and the Institute had a hectic time of it finding people locally who would play host to the young musicians for the duration of the 10-day festival. It meant long and tiring days for them all but the place buzzed with action and they loved every minute of it. Later Festivals included ambitious programmes with soloists such as John Lill (who won the prestigious Tchaikovsky Prize in Moscow only weeks after his Carnegie Hall appearence), Malcolm Binns, Jean Allister, Moray Welsh and the first performance of a specially-commissioned work by Martin Dalby.

During its ten-year run the Festival was well-attended at a wide range of events. There was a lot of folk music, there were ceilidhs, there were White Heather Clubs, puppets and plays. Rep Companies such as Perth and Dundee brought regular drama and comedy and if you look at the programmes now careful scrutiny of the cast lists will reveal small roles for then unknowns like Lisa Goddard and Jill Gascoine.

Local amateur groups put on the likes of Calamity Jane and late-night revues, and real cowboys from Tucson came as a lassoo-twirling choir. Their Director had written the words for TV's High Chapparal, no less.

There was a photo exhibition and Scotland on the Screen, presented by Forsyth Hardy. A Gala Night starred Peter Morrison and Helen McArthur, and there was also the one real survivor to the present day — an Invitation Brass Band Contest.

One Festival exhibition in the Institute Annexe gave the Dunfermline citizens of 1971 a chance to see 'The shape of things that might have been' — a display of plans and designs for some of the wonderful Trust-sponsored ideas that never came to anything, including Washington Browne's 'Carnegie Hall' in the Glen. By the mid-seventies it was getting harder for the Trust to find the cash to get all the musicians to Dunfermline. The miners' strike and the fuel crisis, added to an estimated loss for the following year of £5,000, finally brought the Fesival to an end.

As the Festival was ending its short life, the Institute administration was being taken over by the new District Council. The old Town Council had owned the place since 1965 but the Trust had leased it back and continued to run it for ten years.

(That seemed to be a favourite time span for events. Ten years later an £11,500 estimate for the updating of toilet facilities and other work became a £72,000 bill when dry rot was discovered in the Institute and it had to be closed for some months).

Halls manager Colin Reed warned that Carnegie Hall was about to become an expensive white elephant and, as if to prove his point, pop group Nazareth put on two charity shows to help save the place... and played only to half-full houses.

THE Cowboy Choir who brought a taste of the Wild West to Dunfermline during the 1973 Festival of Music and the Arts. The Tucson Arizona Boys' Choir sang items from the Broadway shows as well as cowboy songs ... and threw in some spectacular rodeo roping as well.

The Carnegie Hall we got instead of Washington Browne's 1,500 seater in the Glen later came in for a bit of a roasting from Billy Connolly, who recorded a live album, one side in Carnegie Hall, Dunfermline, the other in Carnegie Hall, New York. But his transatlantic criticisms of the Scottish theatre brought Dunfermline's Council out in a lather.

After such inflammatory remarks came the real fire ... and a lengthy closure for refurbishment.

FRANKIE VAUGHAN was one of the first pop stars to visit Carnegie Hall ... and his visit upset the then Institute Superintendent, Mrs Cathryn Baxter — before she even met him!

It was all the fuss that was being made about this young man that angered her. Special escort from the ferry by the police, that sort of thing.

However, when he arrived, she discovered an extremely nice man, who seemed genuinely interested in the work of the Institute and all the facilities available for the townsfolk, where children who wanted to learn to play music and didn't have access to a piano could practise there for the princely sum of twopence for half-an-hour.

To Cathryn Baxter, there was a magic in seeing so many youngsters being involved in the junior choirs and orchestras, the elocution classes of Nora Wood and Mary Paterson, the ballet and Highland dancing, and the shows so many of these groups put on every year.

Over a cup of tea, the pop singer listened to the story of some 700 youngsters who paid two shillings a year for membership of the Institute. He asked questions, and showed real interest ... and he won an unexpected fan!

Kenneth Montgomery and the Carnegie Festival Orchestra, 1968.

Carnegie Hall's Gang Show became, in the hands of Jimmy Hunter, the biggest in Britain. One year they took stock and came up with this little list of facts and figures:

180	Members of the 2nd Fife Scouts
60	Helpers doing make-up, scene-shifting, dressing, etc.
500	Changes of costume
222	Costumes made by parents
6	People making and painting scenery for 10 weeks
600	Pages of script
550	Pages of Orchestration
12	Cars and drivers shuttling the younger boys home.

JIMMY HUNTER (kneeling) with the cast of one of the Provost's Command Shows, ten of which he produced and compered. After a gap of a few years, the Command Show was brought back into the Carnegie Hall calendar in 1988.

NO, the Bluebells never quite made it to Carnegie Hall ... but it did boast its very own Bluebell Girl. Audrey Mortimer ran a stage dancing class there from 1974 until she retired this year, with annual shows and her dancers frequently taking part in other shows, such as the panto. Her own connection with the place goes back a lot further ... to a show called Happy Days in 1946, starring no less than Sir Harry Lauder, making a free appearance on behalf of firemen's charities. Her Mum and Dad were both in the show as well. She was taught dancing by Marjory Middleton, at her Edinburgh-based Scottish Ballet School. Later Marjory Middleton set up a Dunfermline section at the Institute and staged pantomimes at the Hall for many years.

In 1950 Audrey went to London where she caught the attention of Margaret Kelly, Miss Bluebell, who put her in a Paris Lido show. In 1960 the show came to Scotland and Audrey appeared with them in Glasgow, alongside Jimmy Logan and Jack Radcliffe. Then she moved to Las Vegas and 11 years as captain of the Bluebell troupe there.

Audrey Mortimer

THE Bluebell Girls didn't quite make it to Carnegie Hall... and neither did the Beatles. This Fab Four were local youngsters taking part in a Gang Show.

CARNEGIE HALL and the Music Institute from the south, looking across the tennis courts which are situated to one side of the new St. Margaret's Drive through the Public Park.

For many regular theatregoers and performers, Bobby Nicholson IS the Carnegie Hall, just as Jack Wright was before him. He first trod the boards in Queen Anne School's Pirates of Penzance and, when he left school, joined Dunfermline Light Opera Club, his first appearance for them being in The King and I.

It ran to packed houses for two weeks, plus another evening and could almost have run forever if they hadn't had to hand back the costumes!

When he wasn't on the stage he was backstage, or up in the gods working a spotlight, or ushering people to their seats. He was an assistant manager with Rank, first in Aberdeen, then throughout the Edinburgh Odeon run of, appropriately enough, The Sound of Music. When Jack Wright retired Bobby became the full-time warden and a couple of years ago he was promoted to assistant halls and entertainments manager.

IN 1982 one of the Friends of Carnegie Hall group visited New York and looked in on the big hall, bringing home to Dunfermline this special medallion which now adorns a wall in the upstairs foyer.

FRIENDS OF CARNEGIE HALL PRESENTED TO THE FRIENDS BY CARNEGIE HALL, NEW YORK, 1982

8

A FRESH START

THE FIRE of 1980 cost a lot more than the actual repair work. Finance had already been made available for the Hall to be rewired and decorated during the following two years so it was all brought forward and the place closed for five months for complete refurbishment.

This affected shows already booked for that period, with tickets and posters already printed and scenery and costumes hired. Sydney Devine moved his show to the Glen Pavilion, but the Corries cancelled, as did the Alexander Brothers, Matt Monro and the Royal Marines.

Probably worst hit, because they were amateurs and couldn't afford such a blow, were Kelty Amateur Musical Association. They were due to put on the Fife premiere of Gigi and a lot of money had been spent on costumes and sets. They had gone for these to a different firm from the one they had usually hired from and found themselves victims of more small print than they had bargained for.

When they cancelled their show they were then stuck with a demand for the full £1,800 hiring costs. Eventually they agreed on half that ... but still had to come up with the full amount again when they did eventually put the show on in October. The only bright spot in it for them was that they got the Hall rent-free second time round.

In October there was a gala re-opening for the refurbished Hall. The Band of the Royal Marines were there, playing everything from Bizet to MacArthur Park, three of Audrey Mortimer's young dancers strutted their style, and then came the Black and White Minstrels, right off the telly, with Margaret Savage leading the singing and Dai Francis becoming Al Jolson before their very eyes!

At the reception afterwards there was a special cake from Marconi, a green marzipan confection designed to look like their Clansman radio, complete with little black tuning knobs. Later it found its way to local old folk's homes.

Soon there was a new skipper on the bridge. Colin Reed left and Lorraine Miller, honours music graduate of Aberdeen University, took over.

She continued Reed's policy of experimenting with every kind of show, again without hitting on a surefire winner except the good old Scots fare. A typical month in the mid-eighties saw performances from the Marines, the Purves Puppets, a Brass Band Contest, the Corries, a Marks & Spencer fashion show, an RSPB film night, a folk night and an old-time music hall.

Band contests were by now bringing in some 30 bands and 700 musicians, and as for never being able to fill the hall, you can tell that tale to the Marines! In the Seventies the Rosyth-based band could pull in 2,500 in Manchester, but just up the road from the Naval Base, Carnegie Hall was not even half full. Now, you can hardly get a ticket for their shows, so successful are they.

Pop was still the Cinderella of Carnegie shows, an extravaganza featuring six bands drawing only 76 people. Perhaps Dundee United's live TV appearance in the UEFA Cup final the same evening had something to do with that! Dunfermline's own Skids had been the last group to successfully use the place and their former keyboards player, Alastair Moore, turned in something a bit different by fronting the Marines band for one performance.

There was another amalgam of two cultures when the Scottish Ballet danced to works by folk singer Dick Gaughan and pop group Jethro Tull. Scottish Opera too came as part of the Carnegie Series of 'quality' concerts sponsored by the Arts in Fife, the Carnegie Trust, and the Scottish Arts Council. Julian Lloyd Webber's cello recital sold out but audiences were sometimes disappointing. And English National Opera Children's Workshop made frequent visits in the 70s, with 90 Primary School children taking 15-minute operas from scratch to performance in the course of 3-hour rehearsal sessions of ENO Producers Peter Kay and Stefan Janski.

SIX months after the fire of 1980, the refurbished Hall opened again with a gala spectacular featuring the Black and White Minstrels, and starring among others Dai Francis as the legendary Jolson.

Radio Scotland broadcast a few shows from the hall, Radio Forth put on shows there, and Arthur Montford brought a round of the 'TV Times' challenge quiz there. Johnny Morris had orchestral backing for animal stories, and Barbara Dickson turned down Carnegie Hall as a venue on her British tour.

She was taken to task for thumbing her nose at her home town but a 'Press' letter writer came to her aid, pointing out that she had appeared there free to help raise funds for a new swimming pool — and the Hall was half-empty.

Her first appearance there was also for charity, but even Barbara may not remember it. It was in 1964 and on the bill in a show to raise money for spastics were The Chorettes, named in the programme as B. Dickson and S. Meldrum.

In 1982 there was a brief remembrance of wartime days when the Task Force Show raised £600 for the South Atlantic Fund, founded to raise money for Falklands casualties.

The following year the Boys' Brigade celebrated their centenary with a show at the Hall under the eagle eye of their President, the Earl of Elgin. Not so welcome was a cash-and-carry sale which led to complaints and a ban on such events taking place there again.

James Moodie would have turned in his grave at the very thought. But then what would he have made of a bodybuilding championship? Or Rupert the Bear? Or Big Daddy wrestling on his beloved concert platform?

Perhaps he should have asked the boss himself? For in 1985 Andrew Carnegie appeared in the Hall — bearing a striking resemblance to Scots actor Russell Hunter — and enthralled his home-town audience with tales of how he made his millions from nothing ... and then gave them away. For more than two hours he recalled his poor boyhood in 'The Auld Grey Toun' and his rise to fortune and fame in the New World.

'Mr Carnegie's Lantern Lecture' was commissioned by the Trust from playwright W. Gordon Smith to mark the 150th anniversary of Carnegie's birth. During its brief run another representation of Mr Carnegie was on view in the Hall foyer — a huge print of an Andy Warhol picture (the original is in the Carnegie Institute in Pittsburgh) which was part of a special display about the man and the continuing work of his Trusts worldwide.

COLIN REED, the first halls and entertainments manager, appointed by the Council after they took over the Hall's running from the Trust. He was manager from 1973 until 1981.

LORRAINE MILLER took over from Reed in 1981 and left in 1986 for a post with the Scottish Arts Council.

CAKE-CUTTING time as the re-opening of the Hall is celebrated. Provost Les Wood does the honours, assisted by (at the back) Vic Crawford, the Convener of Leisure and Recreation, and Mal James, General Manager of Marconi, who presented the radio-shaped cake.

KEN DODD was one of the big stars who performed in Carnegie Hall during 1988, a year which also saw the first full-week run by a professional touring company when Joseph and the Amazing Technicolour Dreamcoat put on nine performances.

THE big freeze of 1981 brought an unexpected stage show to Carnegie Hall ... a christening, in fact **three** christenings! As the Mother Goose panto was ending on Saturday night, Gillespie Memorial Church in Chapel Street were discovering that the heating had broken and there was no chance of it working for the morning service.

So the whole lot ... Christmas service, carols, nativity play ... were moved to Carnegie Hall, where the Rev. Jack Goring happily performed three baptisms on the stage.

A little girl who had to be dragged off Carnegie Hall stage when she was just four years old grew up to become part of the Institute. Wendy Beveridge danced Little Miss Muffet in that debut performance ... and, a born performer, refused to come off when she had finished. After a career as Moxon Girl, the dance troupe who backed the big names of Scottish variety, she started a ballet school in Dunfermline some 14 years ago; it caters now for more than 50 pupils.

It's one of several dance schools in the Institute, others being run by Rhona McNab, Sylvia Henderson, Allana Brown and Sheenagh Crawford.

Dr Magnus Pyke was one of a series of distinguished scientists who were sponsored by the Trust to give Christmas lectures to local school pupils in Carnegie Hall. He talked on artificial and synthetic foods ... and unfortunately at that time he had not become the national 'personality' that television later made him. So his quick-fire delivery and wildly flailing arms as he described something left the children not knowing whether they were supposed to laugh or not.

SUPERB new sound and lighting control systems have been installed. Birthday presents from the Trust to celebrate the Hall's 50th anniversary were a new computerised memory lighting board and an induction loop to help the deaf enjoy shows. The control box (pictured here) was moved to a new position between the entrance doors at the back of the auditorium.

THE permanent annexe which replaced a 'temporary' wooden structure built on the same site during the war... and knocked down only in the mid 1980s.

9

HOUSE FULL

THE opening ceremony of 1937 brought from the Convener of the Trust's Music Committee, William Black, these words: 'It is not the object of the Trust to produce musical experts or even professionals. Their aim is rather the development of amateur talent.' These days, rows over cash for sportsmen have brought the word amateur into sharp focus. Exactly what is an amateur?

In theatrical terms it's simply a person who doesn't get paid for his or her singing, dancing or acting talents. It does not mean that they are anything less than thoroughly professional in their performance or their approach to the job in hand, from rehearsals to the polished final product the public sees.

One of the big success stories of Carnegie Hall's history has been, without a doubt, the amateur companies: the light opera groups, the dramatic societies, the youth groups … doing everything from Gilbert & Sullivan to Grease.

In the Fifties and Sixties some of these societies could fill the theatre night after night for a full two weeks, many of them managing to fit in extra matinees and occasionally a third Monday night just to cope with demand. There was healthy competition too, among such as the Dramatic Society, the Grand Opera Society, the Craig Players, the Randolph Players, societies based in Kelty, Lochgelly, Rosyth … a whole string of them.

Tickets went on sale in places like Muir's music shop in Dunfermline, and local shops in the other places. Queues formed, and tickets were often all gone on the very first day.

Everyone connected with the amateur groups had a mum, a dad, aunties, uncles, cousins, neighbours, workmates, and they all went out to sell, sell, sell! This was part of the fun of being in such a society, just as much as taking part in the production, although sometimes the biggest problem was finding a relative to sell tickets to … they were all in the company as well!

There were members who could sell 100 tickets on their own. Sometimes there was the odd boost to attendance by pupils given free tickets by teacher members of the cast in return for acting as ushers at these happy family affairs.

John Smith, President of Kelty Amateur Musical Association, remembers a time when his company had TWELVE married couples in the cast. He's a fair example himself of a whole family being involved. He's also the producer of Kelty shows, having played leading roles more than 30 years ago: his wife Lena, is choreographer, and their daughter, Mary, who has played leads, including the title part recently in Hello Dolly, has turned down chances to turn professional.

Her husband, Jim Leishman, former Manager of Dunfermline's football team, was the company's business manager and has played a mean gangster in Guys and Dolls, Stewpot in South Pacific, and Red Indians, Black Eagle and Sitting Bull.

Just to complete the generation set, Mary and Jim's daughter, Kate, played one of the children in Brigadoon.

Kelty used to play two weeks every year, using the miners' gala week as rehearsal time: now it's one week. They would put on their shows in the local cinema, spending a night laying a stage extended over the orchestra pit and changing into costume below that makeshift stage.

So when they decided to move their show to Carnegie Hall in 1947 they could only stand and gape at facilities such as real dressing rooms! Maybe though their move was hastened by the time they had a donkey on stage in one of the scenes, and it was right above their changing area, and it misbehaved, and the boards did not fit too well …

Such a thing should not happen on a proper stage, of course … but it did. A Desert Song donkey performed with such gusto that one lady sitting in the front row put her brolly up — and brought the house down!

Rosyth and District Musical Society, which started life as Rosyth Dockyard Operatic Society, are another family group. The President is George Wells, his wife Marie is Treasurer, and they could boast a mother and three daughters in the same cast.

Although the dockyard connection is in the past, many of the orchestra for their shows are Marines bandsmen and at the last Marines concert, three Society solo singers took part.

Little 'accidents' like those involving the donkeys are few and far between … most of the things that go wrong are never seen by the audience. Take the time, for instance, that a Rosyth principal had an accident at work and someone who had played the part a long time before stepped in at the last minute, reading up on each scene just before he walked on stage.

George Wells himself recalls stepping in to play the Star Keeper in Carousel, tending the stars at the top of a long ladder … and reading the words from bits of paper pasted around the top rungs! Another leading performer broke a leg and the choreographer danced on stage while the plastered principal sang into a mike off-stage.

The show must go on … as they say. But when Alex McLennan, who produced some 40 plays in Carnegie Hall since 1949, was hurt refereeing a schools rugby match, there was no way the show would go on with him in it. But that did not mean he had to miss seeing it. He talked his way out of the West Fife hospital for an evening, and was pushed up the New Row and along Park Avenue in a wheelchair to take his place in a hidden corner of the orchestra pit. He watched the show, joined in the meal with the cast afterwards, then was pushed the return journey to the ward.

There was greater public interest in those days in the sort of work put on by groups such as the Dunfermline Dramatic Society. Before armchair theatre came into people's homes, they were quite happy to go out for it. House Full notices were a common sight when, say, a good Agatha Christie was being staged. Shakespeare would not pack 'em in down Dunfermline way, although way back in 1938 Harold V. Neilson's touring company put on no less than eight Shakespearean plays on six consecutive days at the Carnegie Hall.

In later years Shakespearean works and one-act plays were put on in the Annexe, which comfortably accommodated their audiences. The Annexe was ideal, too, for full-scale rehearsals as it was approximately the same area as the main Hall stage. It's used more often now so rehearsals have to go on in more unsuitable places where the chance to really polish a show is more of a struggle, especially for amateurs whose time is limited by the dictates of job and family life.

But even with these limitations, the average member of a musical or drama society puts in a huge number of hours every year, learning, rehearsing, performing, selling tickets, fund-raising … amateurs who are truly professional in their commitment.

Tom Allan is the Hall's official fireman. Tom took on the job before the war at a princely 2s.6d per hour and the 1989 season of shows by the amateur groups was his 50th year there. It's his task to keep an eye on the Hall's fire safety requirements, checking that material on stage is properly fire-proofed, and that nervous actors, having a last-minute cigarette before going on stage, don't forget to put it out completely and in the proper place. But he's perhaps best known, in his peaked cap and dark coat, directing cars outside the Hall, making sure no one dares park where they could hamper rescue services in an emergency.

One area where they have genuine professional backing is the orchestra. For example, after 60 years in the 'pit', Raymond Lyall could hardly be described as anything but professional. But it is with the local amateur groups that he does most of his playing these days. Usually he's leader of the orchestra and he also takes violin classes at the Institute.

By 1950 he had been a musician for 20 years, in theatres, dance halls and on cruise ships heading to and from South America. He moved to Fife and has been involved with local groups ever since.

One major change he has seen in all that time is the slowly-vanishing 'Queen' at the end of shows ... once upon a time none ever finished without the National Anthem, now it is a rarity.

He's been so involved in playing for shows that he can remember actually watching as a member of the audience only one show in all that time. One show remains out on its own in his memories of all the performances he has played for. The Dunfermline Musical Society's West Side Story was 'superb, the finest ever'.

Everything was just right, and there was so much effort put into the fight scenes and the scaling of the back-lot fences and walls that there were actually nurses and first aid personnel in the wings to treat the injuries that happened night after night.

Oddly enough, after such a success, the company disbanded the following year, 1965.

Playing Riff in that production of 'West Side Story' was Alex Wallace, who had been dancing with the Lochgelly and District Musical Association since 1951 and is nowadays their producer.

Lochgelly started in 1935 with shows in the local cinema, just as Kelty had done. Members worked right through the night before their opening performance laying and extending a stage, taking out the first six rows of seats in the process. They didn't move to Carnegie Hall until 1956 and even then it wasn't because they wanted to. They were actually driven to the move by ... Cinemascope. The huge wide screen and the redesigned cinema made it impossible to lay a large stage as before.

They worried about going all the way to Dunfermline because their audience was home-based in Lochgelly. Buses had to take the

A FAMILY AFFAIR: that's the hallmark of many of the amateur groups who make such successful use of Carnegie Hall. Here's just one good example — four of the cast of Kelty's 1978 production of Rose Marie. On the left is Lena Smith, now the choreographer. Beside her is husband John, the association's president and producer, and player of many leading acting roles over the years. On the right is their daughter Mary, a fine actress with main parts such as the recent title role in Hello Dolly to her credit. And behind her, an Indian warrior with a face that might just be familiar if you're local and you look closely enough. It's East End Park's own 'big chief', Mary's husband, the former manager of Dunfermline Athletic Football Club, Jim Leishman.

ALEX WALLACE and his partner Janet Ritchie: their appearance on TV's Come Dancing boosted ticket sales for Lochgelly's Carnegie Hall show.

cast to shows and, as well as the Lochgelly folk who travelled to see the show, they had to start afresh and try to build up a Dunfermline support.

In 1969 they took a gamble on trying something different when they decided to do a Minstrel Show instead of one of the traditional musicals. Initially they booked for only three nights but demand was so great that they did the complete week.

One good thing about taking their show so far from home was that on Matinee Saturdays the evening show always went with an extra swing. There was no time to go back to Lochgelly in between shows so the Co-op did the needful with steak pie teas for the cast ... then it was over to the Park Tavern for what always turned into an impromptu singalong.

> Light Opera Club,
> Dunfermline,
> Fife, Scotland.
>
> January 20, 1955.
>
> Dear Members of the Dunfermline Light Opera Club :
>
> It is with pleasure that I have heard you will be presenting BRIGADOON on the stage in Dunfermline in April.
>
> So it would seem that once more this quaint Scottish village, Brigadoon, is disproving its story which so enchantingly tells us how it comes to life for just one day in every hundred years. BRIGADOON, with the remarkable success it has enjoyed as a musical presentation, must have come to life on a stage somewhere during nearly every day of the past several years. And everytime it has, I am sure, it must have spread its warmth to those performing in it, as well as those viewing the production.
>
> I know that my part in helping bring BRIGADOON to the motion picture screen was one of the most satisfying experiences in my film work, and an experience quite different from any other of my career.
>
> So, on behalf of Cyd Charisse, Van Johnson and all my colleagues, the very best of good wishes from BRIGADOON in Hollywood—to BRIGADOON in Dunfermline.
>
> Sincerely yours,
>
> GENE KELLY.

FROM Hollywood to Dunfermline. Part of Gene Kelly's letter to Dunfermline Light Opera Club wishing them well in their 1985 production of Brigadoon... Kelly having starred in the film version of the Lerner and Loewe musical.

Usually there was a little bit more gusto went into the evening performances, especially the year they did The Student Prince where the big number is the Drinking Song!

In 1976 they moved back to Lochgelly for their Annual Show, to the 450-seater theatre in the brand new Lochgelly Centre.

Before they did, however, there came one of the best-ever 'plugs' an amateur company has ever received. As well as being a principal in musicals, Alex Wallace was also a champion dancer with several TV Come Dancing appearances to his credit, along with his partner, Janet Ritchie. One year they were chosen to do the cabaret spot on the prestigious Carl Allan Awards show on TV, at the end of which hostess Judith Chalmers told all Britain that the wonderful couple they had just watched could be seen again in Dunfermline's Carnegie Hall. Next morning the tickets were sold out!

In 1979 Colin Reed and Bobby Nicholson asked Alex if he would be interested in starting a Carnegie-based company sponsored by the District Council, and into being came the Theatre Guild. They put on their shows in November so as not to clash with other groups. Members joined just for one year — or one show — at a time. This brought in the best players from not only the immediate area but Glenrothes, Bo'ness, Falkirk and other towns. This, though, worked against the Guild succeeding, as there were no regulars in the cast to build up a following. They did only a few shows before the idea was scrapped.

One thing so many of the amateur companies have in common is that their first production was inevitably Gilbert & Sullivan, probably because so many of the shows which have become regulars on the circuit hadn't been written then. So it's a bit surprising to find that the one company devoted entirely to the Savoy operas was formed only in 1971, the brainchild of four local devotees of the style. In addition to their annual show they also put on concerts including everything from Victorian music to Simon and Garfunkel.

While most of the groups were formed around the Thirties, the Choral Union celebrated their centenary in 1974. More than 20 of these years were under the baton of Robert C. Howells, and at each annual one-night performance they have more than 100 singers on

MARY and Bob Paterson as they appeared together in 'The Rose and Crown', a one-act play for a drama festival in the late 1950s.

FOR Mary Paterson the Hall and Institute were like a second home, a place where she was to experience happiness … and tragedy. Mary was a teacher of speech and drama, a section that regularly had up to 300 pupils and put on a show every Easter as well as taking part in drama festivals all over the country.

With her superbly trained voice, Mary graced many a Dunfermline Dramatic Society production.

None was more exciting than the Saturday when, after the final curtain, big Bob Paterson placed an engagement ring on her finger, right there, on the stage. For someone so steeped in theatre, a moment to treasure.

Mary and Bob were married for 12 years, appearing in many shows together, until another show night in 1960, when Bob collapsed on stage with a massive heart attack. Caretaker Jack Wright and fireman Tom Allan grabbed him as the curtain was brought down, but he was dead.

Mary continued to be involved in shows and teaching her speech and drama pupils until she retired in 1984.

In 1989 she completed a half-century of involvement with the Dramatic Society.

stage, extending out over the orchestra pit, the musicians moving to where the front three rows of audience seats have been removed. In 1977 Leslie Shankland took over the baton.

As well as the spring concert they also do a Chistmas one in the Abbey. The soloists are usually professionals and they've had up there on stage with them, Moira Anderson, Bill McCue, J. Mouland Begbie and Clifford Hughes among many well-known names. The Amateur Orchestral Society also celebrated its centenary but did not long survive it.

From the oldest to the youngest, the Hall's own Youth Theatre started in 1981. Elsewhere similar groups are having to cut back the number of performances and struggling sometimes to keep the membership high, but numbers in the Carnegie Youth Theatre keep going up and one of the major headaches every year is to find a production that has lots of principal parts and lots of chorus numbers. While many of the amateur groups complain that young people today aren't interested in the theatre, especially young men, the lads were queuing up to strut like John Travolta in their Easter production of Grease.

Carnegie Youth Theatre put on two shows a year, the Easter one produced, directed and sometimes even written by members.

Tickets for Grease were like gold dust around Dunfermline. A complete sell-out, just like in the good old days of amateur shows. Co-producers of this huge success were two of the young members, one a 17-year-old schoolgirl.

They were not even put out by the fact that one scene demanded a car on stage. They went out and found an old one, arranged for it to be lifted in the side door of the theatre, and that was that. The old stage has seen many strange things, like donkeys, goats and dogs ... but that must have been its first car.

With that sort of confidence and talent around, things can only look good for the Hall's future among the amateurs.

THE Music Institute is a place where teachers of musical instruments and singing can hire out a room, give lessons, rehearse shows, put pupils through exams. Tuition is available in piano, violin, guitar, flute, clarinet, recorder, oboe, accordion, brass, singing and music theory. Dancers have the choice of ballet, tap, Highland and modern stage, with several schools being based there.

More than one generation of Dunfermline children attended the long-established Elocution Classes, sponsored by the Trust and directed by Miss Nora Wood (later by Mrs Mary Paterson), and Miss Helen Veitch conducted a successful Junior Choir. And the under 5s were not forgotten — the Percussion Band run by the legendary Miss Alice Calder and her successors did a lot to instil a sense of rhythm and a liking for music into pre-school age children.

Dunfermline Town Band rehearse in the Institute, as do Carnegie Youth Theatre, the Choral Union, and the Dramatic Society. The Ladies Morning Music Group meet there and there is a playgroup. Dunfermline Arts Guild has for many years promoted an annual series of half-a-dozen winter concerts, ranging from recitals by singers and instrumentalists to dramatised biography, jazz improvisation, and Scots fiddle music.

Others to use its many rooms include the Children's Panel, Parkinson's Disease Society, Fife Alcohol Advisory Service, Marriage Guidance Council, and The Church of Christ.

10

THE FUTURE

The current halls and entertainment manager is Jim McIsaac, who came to Dunfermline from East Kilbride in 1986. Although he's now been on the management side for a few years, his showbusiness roots are in performing. For eight years he was keyboards player with The Section, the band fronted by Chris McClure, now better known as Christian.

LASER beams, hoardings, a canopy with lights all round flashing out what is showing tonight ... it is hardly Carnegie Hall as we know it. Yet these are just some of the ideas suggested for getting the good citizens not only interested in their own theatre but persuading them to go along and help dust off the House Full notices.

There are those, though, who not only frown at such excesses of showbiz razzmatazz, but actively stand against such desecration of its classical facade.

Therein lies the essence of the problem facing halls and entertainments manager Jim McIsaac: the place is suffering from a bad attack of schizophrenia: it just does not know from one day to the next whether it wants to be a red-nosed comic or a prima ballerina.

When he took over in 1986 his remit was to provide a programme of arts and entertainments for Dunfermline District. Since then he has introduced a wide-ranging spectrum of events. Already he has brought in big names like Ken Dodd for two shows, and the professional touring company of Joseph and the Amazing Technicolour Dreamcoat for a full week's run, a bold experiment for a place where, apart from the amateur companies, booking a show for more than one night has been a comparative rarity.

Getting the balance right between the number of performances and ticket prices is an art. A sell-out success can lose money if the big-name star charges a fat fee, while putting the prices up can result in empty seats. Even the successful amateur companies can't afford to get it wrong. A show like Kelty's 'Hello Dolly' can cost around £8,000 to stage.

'If I knew exactly what would sell, unfailingly every time,' says Jim McIsaac, 'I'd be sitting in London right now counting my money!'

PLANS have been drawn for an ambitious new lounge and coffee bar and a £150,000 appeal fund launched. Here manager Jim McIsaac and his assistant Bobby Nicholson examine the plans in detail, standing on the proposed site between the Hall and the Institute, and looking south over the Forth valley.

Opinions on the Hall itself as a showbiz venue vary from a well-known actor once describing it as 'a mid-1920s venue for Sunday concerts' to 'a beautiful little place with a real theatre atmosphere'. One point often made is the difference between that real little theatre on the inside and the staid concert hall image of the exterior.

Recent changes include extending by another week a panto season which had enjoyed 90 per cent capacity over 16 performances and a summer show for an experimental six-Saturday run.

Touring companies are putting Dunfermline on their map and shows like 'The Steamie' are bringing the audiences in.

Two things might hasten a breakthrough. One is better publicity and the other easier access to tickets. In the Sixties there was a wooden kiosk standing outside the old courthouse in the High Street, selling tickets. Nowadays many of the amateur companies take space in the new Kingsgate Centre for the week before their show, catching the eye of passers-by and boosting attendances.

But actor John Cairney said in a criticism of the place: 'A theatre has to be seen to be a theatre. You shouldn't have to go into the place before you know whether or not there's something on.'

In many ways, Dunfermline's relative nearness to major entertainment centres such as Edinburgh, Glasgow and Dundee makes the problems worse.

A half-hour car trip gives locals the chance to hear a major orchestra at the Usher Hall or Johnny Mathis at the Playhouse.

So Carnegie Hall must fight for its audiences. Two tickets for the price of one, family tickets, more advertising to make the townspeople aware that they have their own theatre and that they can see 'The Steamie' or Ken Dodd without having to travel to one of the big towns. Most of all, it must be easy to book for a show, once they've been persuaded it's just what they want to see.

At one stage there was talk of the former courthouse becoming a shopping centre, one of the units being an information or tourist bureau. If that happened there was the possibility of a Carnegie Hall booking unit being installed there. But the whole building was taken over for a lounge bar, shops and offices and that idea died.

Such a site is becoming increasingly essential. The odd thing is that although the Hall and its Institute-based booking office are not far from the centre of town, especially now that the centre has virtually moved up the High Street to the Kingsgate, someone seeing an advert for a show they would like to see will not trek that extra couple of hundred yards along the East Port.

With a ticket outlet in the town they might be tempted to buy there and then.

However, it has to be said that even seeing such an advert in the town is unlikely as the big shops will not put posters in their windows.

Credit card advance booking, allied to bigger newspaper adverts and publicity, and an electronic indicator board in a central position, are among the methods being looked at to attract the public and make ticket buying easier.

That was certainly one of the main complaints voiced by many of those questioned in a survey organised by the Friends of Carnegie Hall, a group formed to promote live theatre in the town. With joint presidents in Iain Cuthbertson and Ian Wallace, they organise hospitality for artists appearing at the Hall, and have produced postcards of the Hall and the Tiffany Window.

The survey also came up with comments that the management didn't think big enough, the place needed a brighter appearance, and there was a need for better sound and lighting.

That latter point was covered a couple of years ago when they relocated the lighting and control box at the back of the auditorium. And a birthday present from the Trust to celebrate the Hall's 50th anniversary took the form of a new computerised memory lighting board, which has made the lighting more flexible and speeded up the time spent on plotting for a show.

An induction loop system was also provided by the Trust to assist the hard of hearing. A new show relay and paging system has put closed-circuit TV screens and speakers in several key parts of the theatre.

Many of these are improvements the audiences never see ... but show quality would be noticeably worse without them.

In that Friends' survey, however, and in comments made over the years by performers and theatregoers alike, one thing has dominated — the absence of bar and catering facilities. It has been accepted officially for many years that this was so and improvements in this area have been Council policy. Only lack of money stopped anything being done.

Now, in their biggest project to date, the Friends of Carnegie Hall have launched an ambitious fund-raising scheme to site a coffee lounge and bar in a vacant area behind the Hall, between it and the Institute. The District Council are likely to match any money raised by the Friends pound for pound and the total cost is expected to be around £150,000. Such a scheme has been on the go since the 1970s but tight controls on local government finances have kept it as just that — a future project.

The fund got off to a good start when the Council decided, despite counter claims for the provision of an Arts Trust and theatre workshop, to allocate £10,000 received from the sale of artefacts from the old Opera House to the lounge bar fund.

The ultimate hope is for open-all-day facilities, bar lunches, lunchtime recitals and performances of various kinds, art and photographic shows in the foyers and corridors and, in the evenings, drinks and snack suppers available before and after shows.

All with the added bonus of having that meal and drink while overlooking a magnificent view down to the Forth, the Bridges and the Pentlands beyond. And there's also the magic of the name Carnegie Hall. Changing it to Carnegie Theatre has been suggested and rejected, and an awful lot more publicity can be gained from the original name, especially among tourists.

It is not everyone who thinks all that's being done are wise investments: some would rather see even more technical improvements such as building a fly tower to allow slicker scene changing, and even better sound and lighting installed. Some feel that money should be spent on bigger and better advertising, or bussing in tourists for a day in Dunfermline, finishing with a Scots show in the Hall at night, or even bringing in a team of PR people to give the place a completely new image. Floodlights, billboards, the whole works. One small snag to that is vandalism. Despite being in full view of police headquarters a hundred yards away, 1987's brightly-lit Christmas tree lasted just one night before it was pulled down.

But whatever is done, or even just suggested, one thing is certain. The place has come a long way from its first highbrow days of James Moodie trying to raise the cultural taste of the populace, when the Trust put on shows geared to a small minority without ever expecting to fill the theatre. They weren't competing on a commercial basis. Some people went regularly to the Opera House, others to Carnegie Hall, rarely both.

If the Trust thought a performer was worth seeing then they put on a show and hoped they wouldn't lose too much!

Those gentle days of yore are long gone. In a world dominated by balance sheets and accountants, anything that doesn't pay is out.

TV and Bingo together killed off live theatre variety shows. But now people want to go out for their entertainment. We're ready for live theatre again.

Ladies and gentlemen, the Carnegie Hall awaits your pleasure.

THE AMERICAN CONNECTION

IN 1959 New York's Carnegie Hall was threatened with demolition to make way for a multi-storey, tinted, aluminium 'box' and the protests poured in. Isaac Stern, the noted violinist, acted quickly. He contacted Mayor Robert F. Wagner and gained his sympathy, and very soon a committee was formed with the sole purpose of saving the Hall.

Supporters of the rescue included Pablo Casals, Leonard Bernstein, Eugene Ormandy, Fritz Kreisler and many other world-famous names from the world of music. Isaac Stern was elected president of the Carnegie Hall Corporation, a position he holds still, and Dunfermline particularly appreciates the message (right) he sent to our Carnegie Hall on its 50th birthday.

The Carnegie Hall
Dunfermline
Scotland

Andrew Carnegie was a man whose generosity spanned oceans -- from his birthplace in Dunfermline, Scotland, to the entire expanse of his adopted homeland, the United States of America -- and, indeed, generations. At the May 5, 1891, opening of New York City's Carnegie Hall, he predicted that the Hall would "intertwine itself with the history of our country." Now, almost 100 years later, it truly has, to a degree that even he could not have imagined.

On the brink of our centennial, we at Carnegie Hall in New York are proud and delighted to extend greetings and congratulations to The Carnegie Hall of Dunfermline on the occasion of its 50th anniversary. I sincerely hope that the link between us will remain forever nourished by a commitment to our heritage, forged by the legacy of the man whose name we bear.

Sincerely,

Isaac Stern

In the last few years the 2,814-seat hall has seen a $30 million restoration to the magnificent state in this picture. What Stern has termed 'an 1890 lady with 21st century plumbing'.